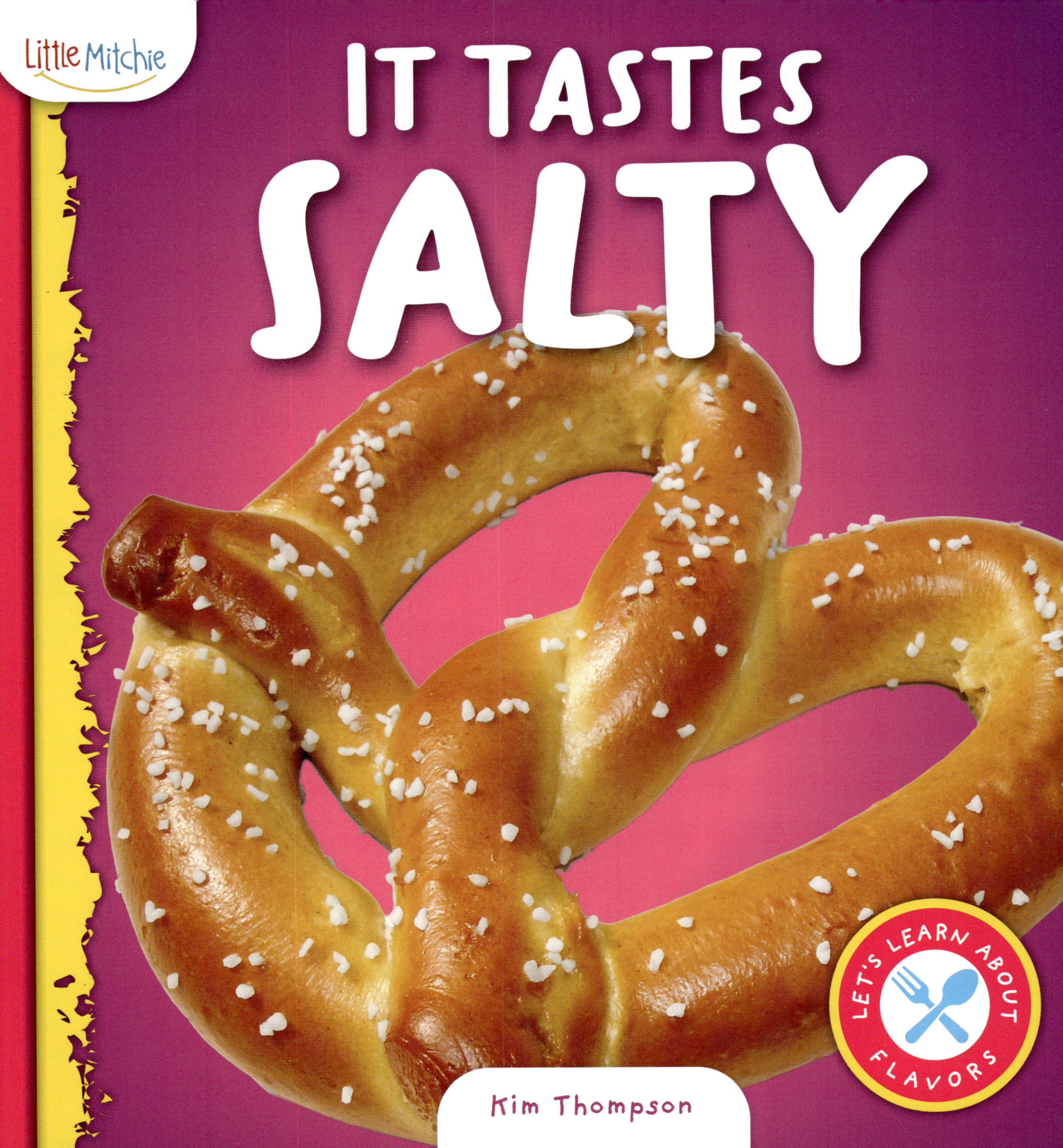
Little Mitchie
IT TASTES
SALTY
LET'S LEARN ABOUT FLAVORS
Kim Thompson

CREATING YOUNG NONFICTION READERS

Little Mitchie books spark curiosity and support early nonfiction reading for students in Grades 2-3. Designed to build vocabulary, support second language learners, and prepare readers for middle-grade content, each book includes helpful tips for parents and educators to build confidence and deepen understanding of the world.

TIPS FOR READING NONFICTION WITH BEGINNING READERS

Talk about Nonfiction

Begin by explaining that nonfiction books give us information that is true. The book will be organized around a specific topic or idea, and we may learn new facts through reading.

Look at the Parts

Most nonfiction books have helpful features. Our *Little Mitchie* titles include color photographs and graphic aids, a table of contents, a glossary, and an index. Share the purpose of these features with your reader.

Color Photos and Graphic Aids

A lot of information can be found by "reading" photos, charts, maps, and other graphic aids found within nonfiction texts. Help your reader learn more about the different ways information can be displayed.

Table of Contents

Located at the front of the book, this list shows the big ideas within the text and the page numbers where they can be found.

Glossary

Located at the back of the book, the glossary defines key words and phrases that are related to the topic. These words and phrases can be found in the text in colored type.

Index

Located at the back of the book, an index is an alphabetical list of topics and the page numbers where they can be found.

With a little help and guidance about reading nonfiction, you can feel good about introducing a young reader to the world of *Little Mitchie* nonfiction books.

Little Mitchie is an imprint of:

Mitchell Lane
PUBLISHERS

2001 SW 31st Avenue
Hallandale, FL 33009
mitchelllanepub.com

First Edition, 2027.

Author: Kim Thompson
Designer: Bobbie Houser

Library of Congress Cataloging-in-Publication Data
Title: It Tastes Salty / by Kim Thompson

Description: Hallandale, FL :
Mitchell Lane Publishers, [2027]

Identifiers:
ISBN 979-8-89260-855-8 (library bound)
ISBN 979-8-89260-952-4 (eBook)

Library of Congress Control Number: 2026935745

PHOTO CREDITS
Shutterstock: Stockagogo Photos, cover, 1, 3, 4, 10, 18; baibaz, 5; evgeeenius, 6; EugeneEdge, 8; Alessia Pierdomenico, 9; Julia Mountain Photo, 11; Pavlova Yuliia, 12; Pixel-Shot, 14; K-FK, 17; Halfpoint, 19; frantic00, 21; DronG, 22.

TABLE OF CONTENTS

Chapter One

A SALTY TASTE

It's movie time at a sleepover. Snacks cover the table. There is popcorn. There are potato chips and corn chips. As you scoop up your favorites, you decide to grab a drink too!

These foods have different shapes, colors, and textures. They have one flavor in common, though. They are all salty!

Some foods naturally contain a small amount of salt. These include meat, fish, and milk. Raw celery, beets, and other vegetables are also a little salty. Even water has some salt in it.

TASTY TIDBIT

Long ago, salt was so valuable that it was used as money. The word *salary* is related to salt!

Most of the salt we eat is added to food. Fast food and **processed** foods are high in salt. Home cooks add salt to everything from macaroni and cheese to baked goods.

TASTY TIDBIT

Salting meats and other foods helps **preserve** them. Before refrigerators were invented, salting food was important for survival.

Chapter Two

THE SCIENCE OF SALTINESS

The substance we call table salt is sodium chloride (NaCl). It is a **mineral**. Salt water from the ocean is full of it. It is also found in rock deposits. The rocks formed when water from ancient seas evaporated and left salt behind.

TASTY TIDBIT

Sodium and chloride help balance the amount of water in your body. They help messages travel along your nerves and muscles.

The surface of your tongue is covered with bumps. These are **papillae**. They are not taste buds. Your taste buds are tiny structures inside the papillae.

Taste buds are shaped like pockets. There are tiny hairs called microvilli sticking out. These hairs sense salt. They send **signals** to your brain. That's how you know you are tasting something salty.

Taste buds detect five flavors. They are salty, sweet, sour, savory, and bitter.

It's not true that different areas of your tongue taste different flavors. All five flavors can be sensed all over your tongue.

Your nose also sends information about flavors to your brain. Tiny particles of food enter the nose. They trigger sense **receptors**. This helps you smell and taste your food.

When your nose is stuffy, it has a harder time doing its job. It is more difficult to taste what you eat.

Chapter Three

EATING SALTY FOODS

People need sodium, but not very much of it. Without any salt, humans get sick. They can become **dehydrated** and die.

Ancient people developed a taste for salt because it was so important for survival. That could be why we **crave** salty snacks!

Today, the challenge is to eat sodium in **moderation**. Too much salt can lead to serious health problems like **hypertension**.

Try to choose low-sodium snacks. Think twice before reaching for the salt shaker.

NOT-TOO-SALTY ROASTED CHICKPEAS

Ingredients:

One can chickpeas, also called garbanzo beans

One tablespoon olive oil

Your choice of seasonings, such as chili powder, garlic powder, cumin, pepper, or a small amount of salt

Directions:

1. Ask an adult to preheat the oven to 400 degrees Fahrenheit (200 degrees Celsius).

2. With an adult, open the can of beans. Rinse them in a colander and pat them dry with a paper towel.

3. Spread the beans on a foil-lined baking sheet.

4. Toss the beans with the olive oil and seasonings.

5. Roast for 20 minutes. Let them cool slightly. Pop them in your mouth and enjoy!

GLOSSARY

crave (krave) to want something very much

dehydrated (dee-HYE-dray-tid) lacking enough water in your body for normal functioning

hypertension (hye-pur-TEN-shuhn) dangerously high blood pressure that makes your heart work harder to pump blood and that can lead to heart attacks

mineral (MIN-ur-uhl) a solid substance found on Earth that does not come from an animal or a plant

moderation (mah-duh-RAY-shuhn) in reasonable amounts that are not excessive or extreme

papillae (puh-PILL-ee) small bumps on the tongue that contain taste buds

preserve (pri-ZURV) to treat food so that it does not become spoiled, often by adding salt

processed (PRAH-sesd) made or changed in a factory; unnatural

receptors (ri-SEP-turz) nerve endings that are sensitive to stimuli in the environment such as smells

signals (SIG-nuhlz) chemical and electrical messages that get sent to the brain through the body's nervous system

FURTHER READING

Highlights. *The Ultimate Science Cookbook for Kids: A Cookbook for Young Scientists That Transforms the Kitchen into a Food Lab for Learning.* Highlights Press, 2025.

Kurlansky, Mark. *The Story of Salt.* Puffin Books, 2014.

ON THE INTERNET

American Heart Association: Sodium Myths and Facts for Kids
heart.org/en/-/media/AHA/H4GM/PDF-Files/Sodium-Myths-Facts-for-Kids_PDF.pdf?sc_lang=en
Get the facts about salt and your health.

Mystery Science: Where Does Salt Come From?
youtube.com/watch?v=WR8GovUng2A
Find out how salt gets to your kitchen.

INDEX